Brazil

Zoë Dawson

RSVP

RAINTREE
STECK-VAUGHN
P U B L I S H E R S
The Steck-Vaughn Company

Austin, Texas

Published by Raintree Steck-Vaughn Publishers, an imprint of Steck-Vaughn Company

A ZOË BOOK

Editor: Kath Davies, Helene Resky
Design: Jan Sterling, Sterling Associates
Map: Gecko Limited
Production: Grahame Griffiths

Library of Congress Cataloging-in-Publication Data

Dawson, Zoë.
    Brazil / Zoë Dawson.
        p. cm. — (Postcards from)
    "A Zoë Book" — T.p. verso.
    Includes index.
    ISBN 0-8172-4013-6 (lib. binding)
    ISBN 0-8172-4234-1 (softcover)
    1. Brazil — Description and travel — Juvenile literature.
    2. Brazil — Social life and customs — Juvenile literature.
    [1. Brazil. 2. Letters.] I. Title. II. Series.
    F2517.D38 1996
    981–dc20   95–10301
                                                              CIP
                                                               AC

Printed and bound in the United States
1 2 3 4 5 6 7 8 9 0 WZ 99 98 97 96 95

Photographic acknowledgments

The publishers wish to acknowledge, with thanks, the following photographic sources:

The Hutchison Library 12; / Jesco von Puttkamer 14; South American Pictures / Tony Morrison - Cover, 6, 10, 16, 20, 22, 24, 26, 28; / Bill Leimbach - title page; / Marion Morrison 8; / Index Editora 18.

The publishers have made every effort to trace the copyright holders, but if they have inadvertently overlooked any, they will be pleased to make the necessary arrangement at the first opportunity.

Contents

All the words that appear in **bold** are explained in the Glossary on page 30.

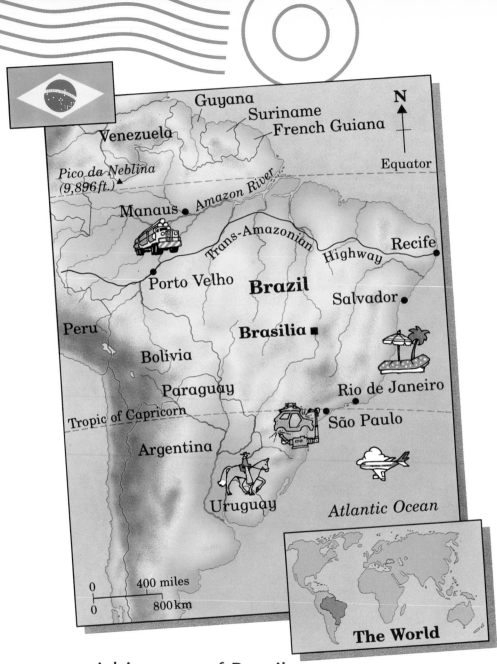

Guyana
Suriname
French Guiana
Venezuela
N
Pico da Neblina
(9,896 ft.)
Equator
Amazon River
Manaus
Trans-Amazonian
Highway
Recife
Porto Velho
Brazil
Salvador
Peru
Brasilia ■
Bolivia
Paraguay
Rio de Janeiro
Tropic of Capricorn
São Paulo
Argentina
Uruguay
Atlantic Ocean

0   400 miles
0   800 km

The World

A big map of Brazil
and a small map of the world

Dear Andy,

You can see Brazil in red on the small map. It is a long way from home. Brazil is the biggest country in South America. We are staying in Rio de Janeiro. Can you find this city on the big map?

Love,

Pat

P.S. Dad says that Brazil is the fifth largest country in the world. More than 150 million people live in Brazil.

Rio de Janeiro and Guanabara Bay

Dear Karla,

It took almost 9 hours for the plane to fly here from Miami. Most people in Brazil speak and write Portuguese. Some people in the big cities speak English, too.

Love,

Susie

P.S. Dad says that long ago people from Portugal sailed to Brazil. They ruled Brazil for more than 300 years. This is why most people in Brazil speak Portuguese.

Copacabana Beach, Rio de Janeiro

Dear Fran,

This is the most famous beach in Brazil. Lots of people come here on the weekends and for vacations. We had a great time playing on the beach!

Love,

Mandy

P.S. Mom says that Brazil is hot all year round. Most of Brazil is in the **tropics**. The middle of Brazil is very hot, but it is cooler near the ocean. Most people in Brazil live near the ocean.

A woman selling snacks on the street
in the city of Salvador

Dear Ben,

Dad gave me some Brazilian money called *cruzeiros*. I buy a different snack each day in Salvador. I like nut cakes and fried **shrimp** best.

Your friend,

Adam

P.S. Mom says that long ago African people were brought to this part of Brazil. They had to work as **slaves**. Some of the snacks here are cooked in the African way.

A small plane lands in the
Amazon rain forest.

Dear Julia,

Brazil is a very big country. The quickest way to travel is by plane. They make big and small planes in Brazil. We went on a small plane to get to the Amazon **rain forest**.

Love,

Carmen

P.S. Mom says that there are many **native** peoples living in the rain forest. They speak their own languages. Some of them also speak Portuguese.

A view of the Amazon River and the
rain forest from a plane

14

Dear Tom,

The Amazon is the longest river in the world. It flows through Brazil to the ocean. A road called the Trans-Amazonian Highway crosses Brazil. This road is more than 2,500 miles (4,025 km) long.

Your friend,

Walter

P.S. Dad says that it would take days to drive to the Amazon rain forest. The trip by plane took only four hours.

A gray woolly monkey in the Amazon
rain forest near Manaus

Dear Pam,

The rain forest is full of plants and animals that I have never seen before. The trees are very tall. People use machines to cut them down. Huge trucks take away the wood.

Love,

Kathy

P.S. Mom says that the Amazon rain forest has more kinds of plants and animals than anywhere else in the world. Many of them will die out if more trees are cut down.

A view of the Neblina Mountains in the distance

Dear Lee,

We have come to see the highest mountain in Brazil. It is called Pico da Neblina. It is cooler in the mountains. There are lots of sheep, but not many people live here.

Love,

Darren

P.S. Mom says that we are near the **equator**. This is a line drawn on the map around the middle of the Earth.

A family on their farm in the south of Brazil

Dear Roz,

Some farms here are very big. Everyone in the family works on the farm. We saw some cowboys riding horses. They are called *gauchos* in this part of Brazil.

Love,

Anna

P.S. Dad says that the best land for farming is in the south of Brazil. Some farmers grow coffee, sugarcane, fruit, and cotton **crops**. Other farmers raise sheep and cattle.

The middle of São Paulo

Dear Pete,

São Paulo is the biggest city in Brazil. There are lots of children around. People buy newspapers and snacks on the streets. Most of the stores are in huge shopping centers.

Love,

Jamie

P.S. Dad says that school starts very early in the morning, when it is cool. School ends early in the afternoon. Some children leave school when they are 10 or 11 years old.

Boys playing soccer in the countryside

Dear Josie,

Everyone in Brazil loves soccer. Children play sports after school. Lots of girls and boys go to dancing schools. They learn a dance called the *samba*.

Love,

Penny

P.S. Dad says that half the people in Brazil are less than 20 years old. They like music and dancing. They are good at many sports. Brazil has one of the best soccer teams in the world.

Carnival in Rio de Janeiro

Dear Sam,

Carnival is one of the most famous **festivals** in the world. It lasts for a whole week. The winners in the parade have the best music and dancers and the best costumes.

Love,

Joey

P.S. Mom says that carnivals are held all over Brazil in February each year. The biggest is held here in Rio de Janeiro. This was the **capital** city of Brazil until 1960. Brasilia is now the capital.

27

Dancers with Brazilian flags,
Rio de Janeiro

Dear Vickie,

The blue circle in the middle of the flag stands for the night sky in Rio de Janeiro. The green on the flag is for the farms in Brazil. The yellow stands for the gold that is found in Brazil.

Love,

Shirley

P.S. Dad says that Brazil is not ruled from Portugal now. The people in Brazil choose their own leaders. Brazil is a **democracy**.

Glossary

Capital: The town or city where people who rule the country meet. It is not always the biggest city in the country.

Crops: Plants that farmers grow. Most crops are used to make food.

Democracy: A country where the people choose the leaders they want to run the country

Equator: The line drawn on maps to show the middle of the Earth

Festival: A time when people celebrate something special or a special time of year

Native: Someone who was born in the place or part of a country that they live in

P.S.: This stands for Post Script which means "to write after." A postscript is the part of a card or letter that is added at the end, after the person has signed it.

Rain forest: Lands that are covered by trees. The weather there is hot and wet.

Shrimp: A small sea animal with a long, thin body covered with a shell

Slaves: People who are bought and sold by other people. Slaves are not free to choose who they work for or where they live.

Tropics: Hot lands near the middle of the Earth that lie on the map between the Tropic of Capricorn and the Tropic of Cancer

Index